Gallery Books
Editor Peter Fallon
THE LAST STRAW

Tom French

THE LAST STRAW

Gallery Books

The Last Straw
is first published
simultaneously in paperback
and in a clothbound edition
on 15 February 2018.

The Gallery Press
Loughcrew
Oldcastle
County Meath
Ireland

www.gallerypress.com

All rights reserved. For permission
to reprint or broadcast these poems,
write to The Gallery Press.

© Tom French 2018

ISBN 978 1 91133 734 8 *paperback*
    978 1 91133 735 5 *clothbound*

A CIP catalogue record for this book
is available from the British Library.

The Last Straw receives financial assistance
from the Arts Council.

Contents

The Last Light *page* 13
Ben Head 14
In a Coastal Classroom 15
Costa Blanca
   COSTA BLANCA 16
   IDYLL 17
   PEÑÍSCOLA 18
   WITHOUT RAIN 19
   FROM NOW 20
   IT IS MORE THAN LIGHT THAT FALLS ON THE EARTH 21
   RETURN 22
Strand 23
Station 24
'It is written . . .' 25
In Kiltane 26
Angler 27
Derrywinny 28
Ómós 29
A Shower 30
'Snow' 31
Father Doyle's Mass for the Dead 32
Church of the Resurrection, Ballinfoyle 33
A Civil Register 34
The First of July, La Boiselle 35
Jo Moran 36
Irish Destiny (1926) 37
Lord Strathcona's Horse at Moreuil Wood, March 1918 39
Unidentified Farriers, Western Front 40
Bank
   DIP 41
   CISEACH 42
   'PEASANT & TURF STACK' 2767.8 43
   TALLY 44
   COVENANT 45
   BANK 46
   NEW LINE 47

    WHERE THE BOG IS 48
    ENSIMISMARSE 49
    LUG 50
    SNARES 51
    A BLIND EYE 52
    LOCKSPIT 53
    STONE TURF 54
    COMPANY 55
Heywood
    'THE BRUTE' 56
    'JOXER' 56
    'NICODEMUS' 57
    'THE BULL' 57
    'THE BUZZER' 58
    'MADAME F' 58
    'SPUD', COUNTY ASYLUM 59
'The Wounded Hussar' 60
Mickeen Cullens, Lisselton 61
Kilcreene 62
The Fourth of April 63
Big House 64
A Rest Stop near Rochester 65
St Paul, MN 66
At Pine Island 67
Heart 68
Keeper 69
Raptor 70
A Mistle Thrush in a Glasshouse in County Monaghan 71
Bird 72
Fox 73
Sisyphus in Cricklewood 74
Two Watches
    JOHN BROCK'S 75
    EDWARD THOMAS'S 75
'Time Takes Care . . .' 76
'The Further In . . .' 77
Tattie Hokers 78
Waiting for the Light to Change 79

'Ourselves' 80
In Killua 81
The Dead of Winter 82
A Conjugation 83
My Brother Sends My Last Book Back to Me 84
The Second of December 85
Kells Printing Works, Maudlin Street 86
The Land Commission 87
After Hours
    SULLIVAN'S, KILLARNEY 88
    MCGINN'S, NEWBLISS 89
    GARTLAN'S, KINGSCOURT 90
    TIGH AN TÁILLIÚRA, CARRAROE 91
    BRENNAN'S (THE CRITERION), BUNDORAN 92
    BERMINGHAM'S, NAVAN 93
    THE CRANE BAR, GALWAY 94
    THE LAST STRAW, BETTYSTOWN 95
A Windfall 96
South 97
Dingle 99

Acknowledgements and Notes 101

for my care

The Last Light

Everything that can be is disconnected.
    Our fire dies. The starlings, nested
in the eaves, have settled. We have cut
    the house adrift to sleep. Now, before

I turn the key, I listen again to my life —
    wind in the roof space, a maternity case
settling on the rafters, waves breaking
    three fields away, a freight train slipping

southwards towards the port; at the stairs,
    our stray stretched out in her shadow;
upstairs, my wife, all my care, asleep.
    Above us, a flight banks in the dark,

beginning its descent. The road, this night,
    goes quiet. I extinguish the last light.

Ben Head

When the red flag is flying at Ben Head
firing is actually taking place.
— Military notice

The gates to *Shangri La* are closed.
    The razor shell trawlers are out in force.
The throes of the old year are over. Like geese
    the pangs of the new arrive on cue —

... *what I have done, what I have failed to do* ...
    From the Refugee Accommodation Centre
sounds of children going about their play.
    A graffiti artist has sprayed on the wall

built for the soldiers simulating war —
    There is somewhere else that is worse than here.
We walk the back beach to the firing range
    and take in at the Head what last night left —

the two duck-down duvets and the *fáinne*
    of stones are a *Toraíocht Diarmuid agus Gráinne*,
their fire gone out before it even got going,
    their single can of cider shared and crushed.

Love thought nothing of sleeping outdoors
    to catch the blessing of the year's first sun.
We'll never know how dangerously they lived,
    sheltering their flame at the edge of the abyss,

risking exposure for one lasting kiss,
    in flight, in love, taking what ease they could,
taking for clouds the snow-covered mountains,
    for snow-covered mountains the clouds just south.

In a Coastal Classroom

'Angels walk into rooms with us. We cannot see them' —
she wrote in the jotter I sign and tick correct and date,
but there will be no more learning metaphor today
because the *cigire* with his metronome has come

to hear the junior orchestra and choir play and sing;
no more for everyone except for this frail one.
Tone-deaf, rhythmless, she gets more English classes
than the others, and loves them, especially metaphor.

The day we opened the windows she wrote — 'The sea
is a blanket the earth is struggling to cover itself with.'
I open the windows to set her loose upon the sea again
as, somewhere in a classroom overhead, the rosining

of bows, throat-clearings, tuning of violin strings ends
as the girls she came to English with break into a hymn.

Costa Blanca

COSTA BLANCA

No solo es luz que cae
sobre el mundo
                — Neruda

A *virgen* beams down on skiffs in the bay.
    I plot my path to the swimming pool by shade
and do my lengths before the heat of the day
    on Calle San Antonio — Day 5. Paradise.

We rise to the migrant dream of Europe —
    air conditioning punctually kicking in,
the coup attempt on a loop on CNN,
    tensions spilling over in a southern state;

Free Movement, an evening tailback on
    the Mediterranean Freeway; nobody coming
demanding admittance with arms at dawn,
    except for the pool man and the groundsmen —

mowers and leaf blowers, a sound of shears,
    the pool left perfect, as if no one were here.

IDYLL

World intrudes on our littoral idyll —
    three streets away a sound like gunshot;
squad cars at speed, sirens, *Guardia Civil* —
    enough to give the children pause for thought.

Here is as good a place as another
    for someone in a strange tongue to declare
to the world where the line in the sand should be,
    flip off the safety, and put us on TV.

The water we came so far to swim in
    is filled, just east, with our sisters, brothers,
dreaming of homes they'll never see again.
    The traditional destinations boom.

If one of these is homeless I am too.
    We'll be home again in our own beds soon.

PEÑÍSCOLA

Remember Peñíscola, that afternoon
    turned monochrome when a bus load of nuns —
some too young to have taken their last vows —
    threw off their sandals to step the hot sand.

Apart from the big beads gracing their waists
    they looked like a flock of seabirds catching
more wind in their habits than seabirds do.
    One amongst them surely must have burned

to leave her habit lying in a heap
    to praise her creator by risking a dip,
to feel the heat of His sun on her back
    and have her faith confirmed by salt and sea.

I blessed my feet by walking, when they'd left,
    the sand that, by their bare soles, had been blessed.

WITHOUT RAIN

As close to the sea as the sea allows
    old stagers, early for the day's campaign,
set out their ice boxes and sun loungers
    and settle for another day without rain,

retreating to the shade they bring with them
    when the sun at midday grows too fierce to bear.
Runners, stripped to shorts and pectoral straps,
    keep to the asphalt and the beaten track.

The Factor 50 ritual begins.
    A parrot alights on a garden palm;
the tiny lizards, liquid among rocks,
    alternate their feet and flit into shade.

Let not my hands have missed an inch of skin.
    O, sun, do not scorch my gleaming children.

FROM NOW

The enterprise of being somewhere else
    goes on full belt around us while we rest.
Northwest, towards our own coast, a *V* of geese,
    taking turns at leading, soars with such ease.

Two nights from now that plane passing over
    will be us — tanned hides gaining altitude,
sand in the places the sun couldn't reach
    in these days of grace that were our lives too.

What better way was there to celebrate
    an anniversary than swimming early
in ocean Homer wrought his epic from,
    and lighting votive candles for our dead,

alive in our thoughts and beyond our reach
    in a stone church a stone's throw from the beach?

IT IS MORE THAN LIGHT THAT FALLS ON THE EARTH

All that week we were lying in the sun
    the fruit of that lemon tree was ripening.
I dreamed of windfalls and thought of the one
    we might slip into a case and fly home

to float a slice of in tonic and gin
    to toast that week away and taste again
the sun and think of that tree, those lemons,
    so close to so much water and so parched.

But their undersides were still mostly green
    and the topmost fruit, holding firmly on,
was showing no signs of coming to ground;
    until, on our last full day — we were alone —

you pointed to the earth and there was one,
    a windfall lying where no wind had blown.

RETURN

Our *Schlüsselhalter* switched on a lamp,
    the one, if we'd been home, that we'd have on.
In the hall, things in need of renewal.
    Our stray has marked all the hours and pined.

The grass grew an inch with the heat and rain.
    The whitethorn quicks we planted came on loads.
Work we set aside waited and increased
    while we learned to operate strange remotes.

In good faith, to this golden place, I came
    (please, Jesus, let me never go again)
to read in the shade, while the good sun reigned,
    that holdall of softbacks the airline allowed.

To our 'Anything strange?' on the road home
    our lift's 'Divil a bit' is all we need to know.

Strand

Let it be solitary
as a cottage on a beach.
— Seán Dunne, *Tea Room*

From the tongue-and-groove of a ruined dresser
    I will fashion shutters for roof windows
to keep the full moon's beams at bay

and give my nights listening to the tide
    felling the sandcastles of a single day
and observe the same hours as the nesting tern.

My closest neighbours will be trawlers,
    fishing for razor shells in shallow water,
who will take my light, that burns to accommodate

their unearthly hours, for a fixed point.
    There will be driftwood for the next night's fire,
dried by the fire of the night before.

The dogs will know me. In the huckster shop
    across the sand all there will be to account for me
will be a list of digits, totted and marked *Paid*.

Station

Some evenings
a nearly empty northbound going through at speed
between the lit-up platforms
leaves me feeling inexplicably bereft,
as if it were my life;

and others
it is the locomotive by itself,
flat out, trying to catch up with
all that went ahead, or going on ahead
to ensure the coast is clear.

It is gone
even before I register its coming.
I am buffeted, buffeted, then stilled.
That is the one that rips the heart from me,
racing, placing all its faith
in one more mile of track.

'It is written . . .'

It is written by the Commissioners that a pauper will pass
a half bushel of bones through a quarter-inch sieve
to keep him and his flesh and blood from starvation,
that those bones will enrich, in their turn, the earth.

The Commissioners' *sieve* is the poor man's *riddle*.
After every half bushel, as the ground around him
grows more and more fertile, a fresh half bushel is found.
But riddle me this — how many half bushels must pass

through that mesh? The same man might crush
the bones of a million animals and more, and still
that sieve will be a *sieve*, and that riddle a *riddle*.

And how can the bones of the hand that holds the hammer
break the last bones to pass through that mesh
when the last bones to pass through it are its own?

In Kiltane

Church of the Sacred Heart, Bangor Erris

I have come again
to do my Stations
before the angel who brings
the water, the bread.

Atlantic sunlight floods
through the lace school's
stained-glass windows.
Whatever I thought

I knew I forgot.
When I leave here
it will be for
the Mountain of God.

Angler

The tape measure disc grows light in his hands
    as he hands the metal end to me to send me
down the road to where the tyre marks end.
    The tarmacadam is a river. He is an angler

and I am the catch being played on the line,
    stopping at a tree skinned of bark, its pale flesh.
He puts some tension on and takes a measure,
    sketches the scene and writes it in his ledger.

These are the clear dimensions of heartbreak.
    This is what it looks like on a ruled page.
This is the record we came in search of.

Winding in the yards, the feet, the inches,
    he reels me back where I set out from,
where the life ended and the death began.

Derrywinny

for Danny Diamond

Maple against his collarbone transforms
clavicle *into a musical term.*

We could be aspirants on spiritual retreat
in Gerry Hennessy's labourer's cottage
where he has done all that he can do —

changed sheets, left turf and food, and moved out
help us to feel at home away from home.
How will we ever be able to thank him?

To do so would be to thank him for his absence.
A tune would be the thing . . .
Trying to write I hear a flight of geese

shedding altitude, heading for Lough Oughter.
The broadband is iffy because of the trees.
The signal weakens as they come into leaf

but he will not allow a chainsaw to touch them.
A week from now this civilized house
will be beginning to become a memory.

You said you felt that music had been played
in Gerry's living room, before his hearth.
The walls and very air contain that feeling.

I would have that said about my own house.
How will we know what to bring when we leave?
We should always be in Derrywinny.

Ómós

for Tony MacMahon

They would be committed
to the deepest bog,
all of the accordions
in Ireland — bar one —

to remind people
of the pestilence that was,
and to dissuade,
by practical demonstration,

anyone tempted to commit
future musical sin.
Then, in a cold church —
the right place for him

to confront himself —
a candle would be lit,
someone would bring
the surviving instrument,

and the master would sit,
strap it on and play
until he had left his pain.
And we would listen.

A Shower

'I am not going to lay a hand on you.
You're going to listen to what I have to say' —
two young men are about to go at it,
hammer and tongs, in the reference section

of the library, among dictionaries
and local history. The one whose people
are from just out the road has had
all he can take of blacks in libraries.

They go outside. The rest occurs beyond
hearing, beyond glass. One talks. One listens.
The heavens open. A great shower
of August rain drenches them to their skins.

'Snow'

for Seamus Smyth

If 'Snow' Gough is doing the talking
    talk of the trenches will be thirsty talk.
'Tell me, Snow, did you ever kill a man?'
    'As many as I've murdered balls of malt.

Most of them were little more than gossuns.
    Every night I close my eyes I see them,
nursing their wounds, crying for their mams.'

Father Doyle's Mass for the Dead

A biscuit box propped on two bayonets
in a hole cut out of the side of a trench
will be his nave and altar and transept.
I offer myself to Jesus as His victim . . .

God's angels in the shell rain overhead,
a chalice in danger of being overturned
when the earth shakes from the big guns
before the altar wine can be consumed.

He holds the God of Battles in his hands
and prays Him to give rest to the souls
of the throng around him, just then killed

or killed the guts of a week, row upon row,
friend and foe, crowding each other out,
then eats the flesh for them and drinks the blood.

Church of the Resurrection, Ballinfoyle

i.m. Anne Kennedy

I know it would kill you to be missing this —
    the priest and the sister above on the altar
who would pass for a couple of ancient lovers
    passing the bread and wine to one another;

an incense boat you'd love to set on water;
    the thurible jingling like a milk float
when you close your eyes, an aspergillum
    creating the effect inside of rain beginning;

he finishes the last crumb and thanks God.
    She puts out the candles with a candle snuffer
or pinches, between her fingers, their tongues.

He loves her. She knows where everything goes.
    Now they bow to the miracle of each other,
to the tabernacle which is their kitchen cupboard.

A Civil Register

So many hearts held on for summer and spring —
    The twenty-ninth of August, '63. Cardiac failure.
The twentieth of June, '42. Coronary occlusion.

I write notes on the printouts for who might care —
    'This is the loss my father never recovered from' —
and prove, repeatedly, to a server being cooled

miles from here, by clicking on jpegs containing
    street numbers, grass, trees, dining rooms where
all of the chairs are empty, I am not a robot.

Catherine. Ellen. Anna Maria. Samuel. Hannah.
    They know the seed, breed and generation of me.
With my own eyes they take me in, my face.

I cross the grass, put my thumb to the latch, enter.
    A chair is brought, a cup passed. I take my place.

The First of July, La Boiselle

Playing war with my brother out the back
    my stone was in flight as he peeped out.
I couldn't have timed it better, and I'd tried.
    He literally did not know what hit him.

As he was considering his stone, its flight,
    it clipped him beautifully above the eye,
broke the skin, encountered bone, dropped
    to the ground and became a stone again;

then the roaring, the disbelief, the shock,
    the rules of our engagement suspended.
His body was all target when he stood
    to take off sprinting, holding in his blood.

I took his life to take the space between us.
    Taking was what made the having worthless.

Jo Moran

A tartan messages bag swung at a handlebar.
Even when the incline forced her to a low gear
her white make-up was never sweated through.
She was a Goth in the time before Goths,
up on her bike from the back end of Clonboo.

Her clothes, and bike, and boots — not boots,
but dainty, dressy, zip-up wellingtons, a touch
of leopard skin at the ankles — were pitch black.
But the strokes of genius that stopped you
were the crawl speed she stayed upright at

and the slash of scarlet her lipstick left.
Fuchsia hardly held a candle to those lips.
If it rained a plastic strip in her hands became
a plastic scarf, and the jaws of her back carrier
unsnapped a cape that unfurled to cover all.

What happened if all that happened was a pension
was counted on a post-office counter and she made
her mark, then half a pound of tea, a bit of meat
for the week, matches and a fuse were bought?
The child she passed did not need to be told

that her travels at night involved no road,
for the sky was element to her then. In her house
you knew that pestle and mortar were in daily use,
that a skillet hung on a hook over flame. You felt
that townlands were patches in her parish's quilt.

Irish Destiny *(1926)*

Other scenes from the film may well have appeared elsewhere purporting to be genuine images of the War of Independence but matters are complicated by the fact that Irish Destiny *is intercut with contemporary newsreel footage of the conflict.*
 — History Ireland, May/June 2010

You wouldn't put it past them to have slipped
a re-cut under another moniker
under the eye of the Board of Film Censors,
but how Eppel's epic ever could've given

Gilbert and Garbo in *Flesh and The Devil*,
Jean Renoir's *Nana*, Karloff in *The Bells*,
von Sternberg's *A Woman of the Sea*,
a run for their money is beyond me.

∽

That single nitrate print of rushes
sat in the vault of the Library of Congress
a blessèd age without turning it,
as it threatened to at every instant,
into a veritable museum of ashes.

∽

It wasn't his stagecraft that landed
Paddy Dunne-Cullinan the lead.
It was rather, they say, because he knew,

from time served as ostler and groom,
fetlock from forelock, wither from poll,
gaskin from stiffle, hock from croup.

∽

So *Irish Destiny* was hacked to ribbons
to earn, as *An Irish Mother*, its censor's *U*,
despite jump cuts every couple of minutes
as iron is unholstered and hell breaks loose.

Lord Strathcona's Horse at Moreuil Wood, March 1918

In St James's Church of Ireland, Athboy,
I accommodate in my lamentations
the horses we hear of from the altar —
combed and loved, bridled and pampered —
which held the line and were cut to ribbons

when they were ridden into German guns;
the few that could, attempting to return
to the place on earth they had last felt safe,
and the one, her tender flesh in tatters,
lowering, among shells, her head to graze.

Unidentified Farriers, Western Front

One has set a shell on a stand as an anvil
    and poses beside it with hammer and tongs
as though he is about to strike a note
    and send them to a man to Kingdom Come,

as another crouches to fashion a cradle
    out of apron and thighs to bear the weight
of the hairy fetlock of a horse whose face
    is the only face we do not get to see.

They have taken time out from the slaughter
    to enjoy the banter and be photographed
by a cameraman who steps from under
    a black cloth and carries their souls away.

Bank

DIP

One slip and you could be breathing water,
    that ruddy stuff running off the high ground,
so you learned to look where you put your foot,
    to think twice about the next step you took.

Once we came upon our neighbour looking
    Olympian in his swimming costume,
flying in the face of all we'd been told,
    taking a dip where the dark water pooled.

His towel hung from a sally. He was swimming
    four strokes and a turn, tipping up his face for air,
and could have been a saint from the Annals

demonstrating to the unbelievers
    something beyond our normal reckoning,
destined to stay beyond our reckoning.

CISEACH

ciseach, f. (gs. **-sí,** npl. **~a**). **1.** Wattled causeway; improvised path, footbridge, over soft ground or drain. *Mil*: **~ chláir,** duckboards. **2.** (In phrases) **~ a dhéanamh de rud,** to trample sth. under foot; to make a mess of sth. **Rinne siad ~ den choirce,** they trampled the oats. **Rinne sé ~ díom,** he beat me into the ground, beat me hollow. **3.** (a) (Of person) Hamper. **Tá sé ina chiseach le feoil,** he is encumbered with flesh. (b) = CIS[1] *1.*
— Ó Dónaill, 1977

How can I tell if it is the sleepers
    or the water they give access over
he intends when he searches for a word
    and finds this one and calls it the *ciseach*?

Because it comes to mean both *bridge* and *stream*
    and it is the only Irish he ever spoke
I have one foot, in my head, getting soaked
    while the other stays bone dry on those beams.

It is closer to what collapses behind,
    to what I imagine collapsing behind,
or to what stays standing just long enough
    for the harvest of months to pass over.

That one word is access and barrier,
    all our firing on the wrong side of water.

'PEASANT & TURF STACK' 2767.8

He has been told how to stand, where to look.
    His jaw is clenched on a pipe stem. He knows
the simple pleasure of a smoke. He gives a fuck.
    His right hand is curled on the haft of a fork,

there for company or to help him steady himself.
    The second finger on his left hand appears
to be pointing, signalling secretly to someone,
    or the bone was broken, set badly and can't be bent,

and he is too old to have it broken and set again.
    He would like to tell the man at the viewfinder
to put his contraption where the sun doesn't shine.

He would like to move one boot, then the other
    till there is nothing but the fork, the stone, the turf.
He will never see this photograph of himself.

TALLY

Now, when I look, I don't know where to look.
    I click and drag a screen and head on out
the Johnstown road, leaving rhododendron
    going rampant abroad in Longorchard;

the Coursing Field, Hallorans, then Geehans
    where the road swings; the fretworked eaves
of the estate cottages where the road begins
    to undulate at Corrig, Derryvilla,

the last two places named, until the ground
    has grown too soft to bear the weight of stone,
and naming here would be a waste of names.

The mapmakers who came here were glad of bog.
    They tidied boundaries, submerged mistakes.
What failed to tally also failed to float.

COVENANT

We are digging out the ground from under
    our own feet, like men preparing the site
of covenant, keeping an eye on the bank
    that leans and towers as we go down,

on a crack that runs the full length of it,
    a fault line in the face of the land itself
that demands negotiation, to be
    accommodated, shored up, buttressed, left.

It has to be worked with and worked around,
    long enough to get the good firing out.
This is the covenant we make yearly,
    the covenant by which we are still bound —

what is the high bank at Easter will be
    deep enough by autumn to drown a man.

BANK

There was a rhythm to the cut and catch.
    He cut. You looked. He swung. It flew. You caught.
He cut. You looked. He swung. It flew. You caught —
    a form of talk that obviated talk.

Work made all speech useless, so the silence
    entered into us and passed between us
and became, with each spit, one spit deeper,
    a ghost bank growing on the spreading ground.

When it came to it in the funeral parlour,
    unsure as yet our job of work was done,
I could not keep my two eyes off him

    and kept, from habit, a *sleán*'s length from him,
not to be caught on the end of his swing
    in case he had one last good swing in him.

NEW LINE

A nailed-up square of tin reads *Carcases*
    out the New Line where the pure bog begins.
I thought of *Morris Minor*s and *Anglia*s
    bumper to bumper, an underwater traffic jam.

I was out the front. I looked into the eyes
    of a white mare trying to raise her head
on top of a load of animals bound for the bog,
    whinnying for her life, wind in her mane.

Maybe she has broken a bone, grown too old,
    or whoever owns her hasn't enough oats.
The stench clears. They call me for my tea.

Even as that trailer turns and gathers speed
    that mare is taking in hedges, trees, fields,
all she still loves with her good heart, in bloom.

WHERE THE BOG IS

It being a name he had never not known,
    when Mac Mathúna asked Pádraig O'Keeffe
on Radio Éireann where O'Keeffe was from,

    without missing a beat he answered *Gleanntán*,
a name that came like a tune or an air.
    But when Mac Mathúna — being Mac Mathúna —

enquired of the master where *Gleanntán* was,
    seconds were an age without a word being said
as O'Keeffe, for what might've been the first time,

    thought about the place he thought of as home;
and in that pause, a *sleán*sman straightened up
    to clean, from the blade of his *sleán*, the scraws,

a whole summer's worth of good turf dried,
    then — 'Where the bog is' — O'Keeffe replied.

ENSIMISMARSE

v. to become lost in thought; to sink into oneself
    — The Concise Oxford Spanish Dictionary, 1998

I knew I'd always known it when I heard
    that perfect, reflexive Castillian,
that verb's infinitive crying out to be
    declined to the ultimate person plural,

for, umpteen times, I had seen it happen —
    a man take an implement in his hands,
measure a bank, strip off the upper layer,
    and strip himself to working boots and pants,

then start to go quiet as he went down
    until he found himself standing in something
akin to a chamber without a roof
    where the only threat was the threat of water,

to which he'd become perfectly attuned
    because he'd dug to the centre of that room.

LUG

I was too slight to bear the weight of it
    and lacked the knack to ease that ash lug down,
yet he let me stand in his place and take
    the weight of his blade while he stood in mine,

his huge hands empty for a change, held out,
    prepared to catch and load what I might throw,
while I closed my two hands on that handle
    and took in what was always in his sight —

the flat ground behind, darkened with our work,
    that undulating road we'd driven there,
everything in the foreground expectant;

and all that strength I'd taken for granted,
    lightness of touch and counter-balancing,
being borne in upon me by that ton weight.

SNARES

You might take him for a chap setting snares
    the way he scrambles about on the high bank
connecting speakers to a wireless
    with cables stripped to their coppery ends

and wound to the coils of a big blue battery,
    searching the air for the best reception
to broadcast on long and medium wave
    to whoever is working the low ground,

in the hopes of hearing, not the forecast —
    for the weather is the only thing we know —
but what comes directly after and before,
    the music of the moment — Young, Lynott,

Heart of Glass, AC/DC, that demented
    schoolboy deep in a reverie of pure music.

A BLIND EYE

for Sadie Mackey

We were dropped off and sorted into groups
    when we hunted hares there. I remember
the strangeness of passing, with strangers, through
    a place I knew every hump and hollow of.

There was the circle where we boiled our kettle,
    marks on the bank my father's blade had made,
scythed rushes spread on the spreading ground,
    marks of our *Bushman* on sallies we'd cut down.

We'd come to drive the hares from their deep forms
    into nets the men had gone ahead to stake.
I nearly thought I'd see ourselves at work
    and this was what it meant to be at odds —

to feel a stranger in that place I knew,
    and turn a blind eye to what I was not blind to.

LOCKSPIT

n. a small trench opened with a spade or a plough to mark out the lines of any work, supposed to be derived from Locus-pit.
— Ogilvie's *Imperial Dictionary*, 1850

The one who'd dug it was feeling no pain.
    It was more boundary than double ditch
or wall, buried between duckboards and drains
    by heather in the middle of nowhere.

It had been approved by ones who maintained
    maps and deeds and rights at some remove,
where the past tense of 'throw' was not 'trun',
    and 'hommer' would not pass for 'hammer'.

It was bound up in the town with fine twine.
    Insistently, in its low whisper, it spoke —
'Thus far will you go. And no farther.'
    You could step over it and keep going

and never have it dawn you'd crossed a line.
    If you put a foot in it you'd break bone.

STONE TURF

Measured by eye and nicked out of water,
    when it slid off the *sleán* and came at you
through clear air at Easter it was pure water,
    freezing catchers, working the *sleán*sman hard.

Wind and sun could reduce it to nothing
    but, given the right amount of both,
it was black gold, as heavy and as hard
    as stone that burned in the range like coal.

So a keen eye was kept, and it was handled
    and borne out over a bridge of sleepers
that threatened every year to give under it.
    And every year, without fail, it was worth it.

The trove that was sweated over and sun-burned
    acquired its name, became what it was called.

COMPANY

A lifetime off the bog, it stands to me —
I learned to be lonely in his company.

Heywood

Genio loci quieti sacrum

'THE BRUTE'

He barrows hundredweights of dung
in daylight across the Quad to feed
roses in Lutyens' sunken gardens,

and passes in darkness between
the rows of our beds, watching over our sleep,
making of us his night roses.

'JOXER'

Our one and only elocution lesson —

our English master, who'd tackled
rats as big as cats on the Missions,
armed with nothing but a wire hanger,
went around the room singling out

boys from Wolfhill, Spink, Attanagh,
Timahoe, Ballyroan, The Swan,
who left hand skin on the walls
when they played handball,

to pronounce 'horse hair' as 'ho'se haaa-ai'
and moved, after Liam Whelan's
woeful rendition, swiftly on
to *Paradise Lost*, Book One, page one.

'NICODEMUS'

Living proof, with setter to heel
and ash plant to hand,
patrolling smoking haunts,
the perimeters of the known,

that the appetite for discipline
is diminished not one whit
by having three quarters
of the digestive tract removed.

'THE BULL'

In a music room converted from stables
mangers become music stands,
and *piano, piano, sul, sul, tasto*
is what you say to calm a colt.

I take my trumpet out to the handball alley
to hear myself play the first notes
of 'The Last Post', and be blown away
when the older Casserly

stands up for everyone when he
stands up for himself when he
interrupts his music master's overture —
'Would you ever fucking cop yourself on?'

'THE BUZZER'

He has been writing
to the broadsheets for years
on matters of Church teaching.

I have seen him close,
in a cold rage, the bones
of his hand into a fist

to correct a child
full in the face
and leave him

in a heap on the floor,
before returning,
without missing
a beat, to his thought.

'MADAME F'

It is not — not just — her lifting
her hippie skirt over a castored heater
in a prefab in the depths
of a midlands' winter,

but the stick of chalk she lifts
and angles to the board,
that new tongue flowing
from her freckled hand,

the chalk column diminishing
in a chalk mist, that causes me —

as it caused me then —
to fall out of my standing.

'SPUD', COUNTY ASYLUM

A man smoked by a fire extinguisher.
A tiny, white-haired woman, lifting her shift,
told Seamus Murphy that he was a beautiful girl
and that he had the most beautiful hair.

I saw her palm resting on his face
as we leaned on deep sills and talked weather
with people who hadn't been outside in years,
and Seamus, gentle, not fending her off.

He had the most beautiful hair in the world.
It has taken a lifetime to take her at her word,
to count her tender touch among the Mysteries
Brother François gave out on the road back.

'The Wounded Hussar'

I want the morning to be akin to this one,
    clear and cold, the first calm maybe after days
of storm; for rumours of snow to be in the air,

    so that the sight of flames will warm the hearts
of the handful there; for 'The Wounded Hussar'
    to be played, once, the way MacMahon plays it;

for there to be time for everything, no urgency;
    my sons to be stationed at the piers on the way in,
pouring shots into glasses arrayed on trays from tall,

    gold bottles of *Powers,* the way my father's people did
at the gates in Kilmacabea; and for a scattering
    of my poems, the ones that meant the world to me,

to be read over me by somebody who knows —
    as I would read them — clearly, without show.

Mickeen Cullens, Lisselton

1st Battalion, Royal Munster Fusiliers

Not wanting to be drawn on the subject of war
    nightly you charge in the second wave
in your bed in the County Home in Killarney
    through what remains of the Bois de Wijtschate

and come upon none other than Paddy Kennelly,
    busy drifting in and out of consciousness
as he bleeds to death and calls out to you
    to risk being shot yourself by shedding

tunic and shirt to stuff into his wounds,
    then bearing him to a dressing station
and giving him a second chance at life

    before returning to the fight, half naked
and freezing, whimpering and sweating
    in the no-man's-land of your Kerry bed.

Kilcreene

This is the bed he will not get up from,
    even when we come to bring him home.
He is sunk in the depths of his suffering
    and steps from pants legs in the cubicle

where I am on my knees to lift them clear
    of his feet so that he does not stumble.
I gather his nudity in my arms
    as I gather his clothes and walk with him

to the bedside and watch as he lies down
    for nurses to attach weights to his ankles
and hang them on pulleys over the end.

    I know now this is how a god lies down.
I kiss his stubbled cheek, his handsome face,
    and bear, in shopping bags, his clothes away.

The Fourth of April

All the accoutrements of hospitality
    graced a table that made scones look huge —
pristine Willow Pattern depicting love,

    fresh tea in a pot cozied on its stand,
jam from wayside berries in ramekins,
    cream whipped in a pewter jug and transferred.

In that perfect absence of running water
    I fancied I could hear a cold tap drip
as the violin kept its silence on a nail.

    The only thing I could think of to say
was Seán Dunne's lovely poem about the place
    and I had in my head as I rose to leave

two tunes that needed only verses and airs —
    'The Boesinghe Polka'. 'The Winding Road to Slane'.

                               Janeville, 2014

Big House

That noise is not the noise
                         of cutlery, *bon mots*;
that's Dinny in the dining room,
                                turning the oats.

A Rest Stop near Rochester

Buzzards are returning to the hard shoulder.
    The strapped State is letting nature handle
the road kill we encounter heading south —
    skunk, deer, raccoon, wild turkey, no badger.

We read 'A Blessing', cast in resin, blessing all
    whose absences are perfectly preserved
by a caretaker making circles with a cloth,
    moving from one picnic station to the next,

a Zen master in overalls observing
    his silence in this temple of departure.
Before belting up to hit the road again,
    in restrooms kept so clean it is as if

nobody ever stopped to pass water here,
    we leave no trace and dry our hands with air.

April 2016

St Paul, MN

A deft, bare figure took a stride toward me
    in a nightmare on the outskirts of St Paul;
then, as if hell-bent on dance, it linked me
    and, stepping again, pressed its spine to mine.

It hooked my other arm and dropped to earth,
    wearing my body like a knapsack then.
Its whole front lay in contact with bare clay
    and I was face up, incapable of movement.

It began to send its sound up through me,
    a groundswell that entered the empty space
in me and made the marrow of my bone vibrate.

    I bore it for an age for want of choice,
absorbing it by keeping my mouth closed,
    until the sound that left me woke the house.

20/21 April 2016

At Pine Island

for James Silas Rogers

Duffy's Farm is as lost on the farmers
    in *Hardware Hank's* as it is in the mists of time
and the Hutterite man, paused at the crossroads
    on his *Muddy Fox*, does not know how strange it is.

A block from the History Center, youngsters
    edging their grass, are mystified by our pilgrimage
and send us to talk to grandma who goes into
    her memory as into her house for a name or a number.

How will we account, when we pass through Customs,
    for the sliver of stone we brought from the old house?
I hope our children, when my time comes,
    will build it into a wall and make sense of it.

This is how beautifully it happens, James —
    with strangers amazed at how far we'd come
we came to stand between ruins and land where,
    a hammock's length apart, the two pines stand.

Heart

I have counted myself amongst the ones
    shitting their linen in shallow trenches
at the prospect of walking into guns,
    of being clipped before they clear their lines,

being roused at cockcrow to be relieved
    of pocket books, last testaments, field wills,
to have a page from a notebook ripped
    and safety pinned like a confirmation badge

or shamrock to the left side of their chests,
    to indicate the whereabouts of their hearts
to brothers-in-arms, selected from the ranks,
    who compensate for crosswinds, draw a bead

and keep, as they stare into the crosshairs
    at that chit, their own eyes clear of niggling tears.

Keeper

i.m. Leigh Richmond Roose

The goalkeeper may, within his own half of the field of play, use his hands, but shall not carry the ball.
— Rule 8, The Football Association

He is advancing with the ball at his hands
into no-man's-land, risking his clean sheet
to let the centre halves know he's there,

shoulder-charging wingers, speed merchants,
launching attacks into penalty areas,
bearing down on the opposition keeper.

He is putting his body on the line,
the fear of God into penalty takers.
He is propped on the crossbar, spinning yarns

to whoever in the stands might lend an ear.
That's a magnum of bubbly by the post.
He doesn't miss a trick. He's everywhere.

He is like lightning when he goes down.
The shot that beats him is out of this world.

Raptor

It had plotted a flight path through our room
    into the garden to the corn field behind,
but drew up short at the living-room window

at the last split second before impact,
    its wing feathers fanned to their full extent
to save itself from shattering against glass.

That glimpse of what it took for a raptor
    in full flight was what stopped it in its tracks.
It rested briefly, then, in the apple tree,

throwing an eye around, settling its mind
    on its best move. On the next up-current
it swung, without trying, into clear sky

as my heart in that room, like prey reprieved,
    flailed and flailed at the ribs of its bone cage.

A Mistle Thrush in a Glasshouse in County Monaghan

I could not say the hands
                      I made into a cage
to bear it out grew
                      emptier when I
held them from me

to let it fly, just that
                    what they held
became more air,
              that I, by its
wing touch, touched sky.

14 June 2017

Bird

Men who hadn't drawn a breath in years
    were drawing wages, paying union dues.
We were living two lives, between houses,
    rising at evening to sweep floors, fill skips,

loading every second one with scaffolding
    and flogging them to scrap men for sterling.
Like every other mother's son in *The Ten Bells*
    I had my own name and the name I answered to.

I saw, in the small hours, a man lose a hand.
    It plummeted ten floors. I learned the sound
of a grown man roaring for his own limb.
    They managed to reattach it. He worked again.

I took it, in mid-air, for a bird. The fall,
    I heard, broke all four fingers, the thumb.

Fox

The Silver Fox is reaching down a hand
      to help me to my feet at 23rd and Lex.
We'd been shifting a bench saw when the flex
      got yanked and stripped, and I took the brunt.

He is checking now if I am concussed —
      'What day of the week is it today?'
'How many fingers am I holding up?'
      'Who is the President of the United States?'

A curlew sings. A skylark hangs in air.
      'The President of the United States is . . . '
The parquet under me feels like heather.

I will reach to take the Fox's hand as soon
      as I have dug this last spit to the last.
The day of the week is anyone's guess.

Sisyphus in Cricklewood

He was sitting on the end of his bed
    in a no-frills B&B off Oak Grove,
smoking a roll-up, addressing the dark.
    He might've been after a nip or two.

He'd been painting the one bridge for years,
    working his way from span to span, turning
a blind eye to the torrent of the Thames,
    stopping to eat and smoke and study form.

He'd been fresh off the boat when he began.
    An old hand showed him the ropes early on
and left him to it when he'd got the hang.

    Now he does it most days with his eyes closed.
Each new year he sets out for the far bank
    and, each new year, for the far bank again.

Two Watches

JOHN BROCK'S

Presented by the Magistrates to Constable Brock on the occasion of his volunteering for active service, December 1914.

The glass of the face came back from the Front
    without a scratch, as perfect as the day it went.
The grandson of the jeweller who sold it
    opened it to service it and found it

not so much stopped from being over-wound
    as empty of hour and minute wheels, yoke spring,
winding stem and end plate, the hands joined
    like hands in prayer, eternally at ten past two.

EDWARD THOMAS'S

7.36 a.m. Central European Time

This is the time in France.
                            The time it takes
to take in the shadow an hour hand casts
the instant it is changed to a sundial,
the first faint signs of rust on numerals,

an imperceptible ripple in the face,
and to imagine its inner workings,
is the interval that happens between
one breath
            and the breath that follows it.

'Time takes care...'

after the Irish, ascribed to Eoghan Rua Ó Suilleabháin (1748-1784)

Time takes care of, and gales destroy,
    names that had weight — Alastair, Caesar;
only grass lays siege to Tara and Troy;
    why, even the *Sassenach* himself might die.

'The Further In...'

The piper who marched into the cave
in Maghera with his collie by his side,
playing 'The Further In the Deeper',
or the skeleton of the tune that came

to be known by that name, went all the way,
whatever 'all the way' is meant to signify,
his flurries and quavers growing more faint,
never to be heard of in this world again.

Days later, blinking the way you do when
you're used to dark and you come back to light,
the dog wandered out, although 'dog' might

be overstating the matter, since it was
without fur and skin it returned, without
so much, fixed in its jaws, as a chanter.

Tattie Hokers

The Seaforth Highlanders have paused to help
    a farmer on the road from Amiens to Albert.
It is tattie-hoking time. They can't resist
    stacking rifles and throwing off backpacks

to postpone death by bending astride drills
    and bearing the ache in hamstrings and backs
as they handle the turned earth and caress
    a handful of the yield one hand digs up

while the other digs in to turn up more.
    There's talk of them tasting like balls of flour.
Mucking in here makes it peace time briefly.

The scent of potatoes brings back the bothy,
    straw mattresses arrayed on seed boxes,
the cow house swept out for men to lie down.

                      Amiens-Albert, October 1916

Waiting for the Light to Change

On a street corner in The Village,
waiting for the light to change,
the painter Beauford Delaney

points to the ground and tells
his friend James Baldwin to look,
who looks and sees only water

until Delaney says, 'Look again.'
And when he does he sees
oil on the surface of the water

and the city reflected in it.
That was the moment he saw;
the light changed, and they crossed.

'Ourselves'

Those were the first months after the worst had happened.
It was early evening, the hectic time when she would be
flat out, and the range belting out heat, but she was sitting
like a visitor in the sitting room in an armchair of the suite,

reaching up a hand to me where I was, over by the door,
about to leave the room. I took her hand and, as I did, she said —
'We all have to look after ourselves now.' I didn't know then
that she was saying she'd done all she could, that this thing

that had come amongst us was too much, that what we had
known up to then was finished with. This was the new life.
All I could be sure of was that she had made no mistake.

She hadn't meant 'each other' and let 'ourselves' slip out.
I picked at those words to get them to mean something else,
then gave her back her hand and passed from the dead house.

In Killua

John Gavin showed me the blacksmith's mark
pressed into the top bar of the graveyard gate,
like a thumbprint, before the iron cooled; the grave
of the priest-hunter Courtney, the tree Courtney's men

hung good Father Barnwell from; the roof slate
that was a headstone he pulled scutch back from
to read the name and date scratched with a nail;
the ice-house built into the side of the hill;

the pile of stones that was the house where lords
of the manor claimed their *droit de seigneur*;
a lime tree named *The Pride of Killua* six men

holding hands could not span. Who will know
these things now he is gone? Who will play
'The Long Street of Ráistín'? 'The Lonesome Road to Delvin'?

The Dead of Winter

for Ruth

He has climbed in
and fallen asleep
at his grandparents' feet

in Reilig Mhuire where
no sound on earth
will waken them.

The living are so good,
bringing everything
the dead might need —

dreamcatchers, tied
to the birches, catch
the dreams of the dead;

the wind chimes play
all the tunes that come
into the wind's head.

A Conjugation

for Bill Coleman and Orla Kerbey on their wedding day

from the Latin 'conjugatus', literally 'to yoke together', hence 'to marry'; join together especially in pairs; having the same derivation and therefore some likeness in meaning; of two leaves of a book forming a single piece.
— Merrriam-Webster Dictionary

It makes, today of all days, perfect sense
    that you should conjugate the Present Tense
'for unchanging situations, general truths' —
    I do. You do. He does. She does. They do;

the Simple Present too, for what is simpler
    than that short phrase abiding forever,
and that infinitive being declined to speak,
    in a single breath, of love and honour.

Live all the implications of this present.
    Take all they mean, absorb them as they come,
and conjugate them to your purposes.
    In tandem and in equilibrium,

as the two leaves of an open book, be
    yoked, alike in meaning, a single piece.

My Brother Sends My Last Book Back to Me

'I was *there*. I don't need to read about it.'
    He doesn't even need a fresh envelope.
I would thank him. Lord, I would thank him.

He's only gone and done what I would do,
    put distance between himself and the book.
I would post it in an instant, but to whom?

These stitched and printed pages I have lived
    send me outdoors to grieve among trees,
this death that, through my door, has just been slipped.

The Second of December

The buses have stopped running.
The text that arrives in the evening reads —
'No operation. Chemo starts tomorrow.'

I walk two miles bearing the evening meal
in a rucksack on my back, and a stone
of potatoes in a bag in my hands.

Flight after flight of starlings head east.
I stand to listen to their wingbeats,
to watch, out the back, filching the last

apple, a rat in the stunted apple tree.
No flights are leaving. The sky is quiet.

Kells Printing Works, Maudlin Street

after the photographs of Suella Holland and Stephanie Daly

The world is set to rights by things continuing
to be where they have always been. Here are
the worn-out vowels and pristine consonants;
there yet, the last print job, set up, pending,

since the last printer turned the key forever.
Here is a whole language we do not speak
of women's names he knew his presses by —
Jessie, Jezebel, Daisy, Penelope, Biddy.

Everything here means something other —
'devil', 'bleed', 'spine', 'orphan', 'tip', 'proof'.
Words we thought were our familiars become
as strange as words we have never heard before.

Crossing this threshold we leave the world
and enter another, to look, touch nothing.
Here is a chance to be reduced to silence.
Here is a chance to learn to speak again.

The Land Commission

Most had never been further east in their lives
than the City of the Tribes. She cried every mile
of the road on the bus they strapped the roof timbers
of the old house to, because it wasn't right to see,
like tiny fields, those clay floors open to the sky,

and hardened, in time, for the children's sake, her heart.
In his ninth and final decade, if you ask him,
he'll say the thing he missed most, and misses still,
is the mountain commonage that he learned
every inch of as a child, where they fattened geese.

She didn't believe the fish the merchant brought
to Stamullen could be fresh, coming as they did
from far Balbriggan, because the sea, a stone's
throw from her own back door in Roundstone
was where she was accustomed to keeping them.

The old man resigned himself to being buried
among strangers. Her daughters are her fortune.
Wherever they sleep — Glasgow, North Dakota,
Philadelphia — they answer her in their first tongue.
To the back doors of their dreams the sea comes.

After Hours

SULLIVAN'S, KILLARNEY

At the hour and date mentioned I was drawn
    to a door by the sound of a cork being drawn.
Kneeling to look through the post slot I saw
    Miss S draw, from a dark bottle, a second.

The light was good in the shop; the door closed.
    Seeing nobody except the aforementioned
I kept my eyes to the slit in the letter box,
    then knocked and called on her to open up,

whereupon all light was extinguished in the shop.
    I could see no more. There was no word for minutes
until Miss S called to her sister for a match.

She opened up. The drawing of a cork is no offence
    yet none was ever drawn without a purpose.
The only steps I registered were hers. I entered.

    Killarney Echo and South Kerry Chronicle, 28 June 1913

McGINN'S, NEWBLISS

We know it is because the back door is open
    that there is a draught and still,
every time the wind pushes the side door open,
    Fiona, my drinking companion, says —

'There's Annie again' — and shows me how,
    towards the end, when Annie could barely stand,
she passed the pints she'd pulled
    across the counter using her two hands.

It is a description of pure spirit
    and I could nearly cry. The new owners
are going to keep things as they were.

We have one for the road and then,
    because we can think of no reason not to,
we make up our minds to have another one.

GARTLAN'S, KINGSCOURT

Ranged beneath a sign that reads *Cosmetics* —
    Dove, Cif, Fairy, Brasso, Sure, Ajax —

and on a salvaged counter top, the scales
    where all that's weighed are the sun's rays.

We are keeping the non-perishables company —
    a *Regentone* wireless, a wheel off a *Model T*,

lines by local scribes, prints of the Fair of Muff —
    in the hopes that their essences might rub off,

while we kill time with each other's confessions,
    drops of water, small ones, the same again.

TIGH AN TÁILLIÚRA, CARRAROE

It is mid-morning and we are waiting
    for the bus in the lounge in Carraroe.
The other customer, sitting at the bar,
    stands and dances to a jig on the radio,

his ox-blood boots scuffling the lino
    until the tune ends and he sits again,
raises his glass and finishes his drink.
    The bus pulls in. We load up. We go.

That was thirty years ago. I have seen
    men in the throes of dancing since,
but none like that man that morning,

who stays with me not because he was blind
    but because he did the only thing he could
when the tune came on. He stood. He danced.

BRENNAN'S (THE CRITERION), BUNDORAN

i.m. Nan Brennan

To be born in a room above the bar
    is to never not have been within earshot
of talk rising like heat through floorboards,
    of a voice saying 'time' and 'please'
gently, as if requesting a little more.

BERMINGHAM'S, NAVAN

Spirits ranged before mirrors on high shelves,
    and us, taking the shyness off ourselves.
Any minute now somebody is going to repeat
    Nell Smyth's story of the ghost coach-and-four

and the night they kept her up to hear it,
    and we will listen, and think, and drink deep.
Reflected amber; time stolen, reprieved;
    one tap whispers, and another agrees.

THE CRANE BAR, GALWAY

Nobody has anything to say
    to anybody else who is there.
Mid-afternoon. A handful of souls

pacing themselves, minding their business.
    It is overcast and rain is promised
or it is horsing down in buckets.

A woman stands and announces —
    'I won't go back to Limerick,
and nobody can make me' —

then resumes her seat, her drink.
    And we, in our silence, drink
to not going back and raise,

in our hearts, our glasses
    to nobody being forced to go
anywhere they do not want to,

until peace reigns again
    in the whole of The Crane Bar
and in The Little Crane.

THE LAST STRAW, BETTYSTOWN

Six Happiness was always *Six Happiness*.
    But what was *The Last Straw* called before
it became *The Last Straw*? If the licence
    is going the bookies can't be far behind.

On the landward side a plywood sign reads
    The Beach View. They'd live music at the weekends.
Hazel O'Connor played there. You couldn't move.
    'Behold what I have done. I've built a better world

for everyone . . . ' Earth movers and a wrecking ball
    will reduce it to what it was, a fork in the road.
A household out for a Sunday spin will slow
    for someone who can just about recall to go —

'I saw your woman here . . . help me . . . that song,
    "World without end . . . " . . . it's gone . . . it's gone.'

A Windfall

> . . . *when a barrage balloon was seen floating very low . . . men weeding mangolds were so affected that they pulled the mangolds and left the weeds after them.*
> — *The Southern Star/Realt a' Deiscirt, 12 August 1944*

It'll never happen now, that windfall poem
about the shotgun kept for thinning out crows
being taken down to shoot down one amongst

the barrage balloons tethered along our coast
to put some halter to the *Luftwaffe*'s gallop
during my father's seed time in Ballyroe,

because the material they were made from
was made for keeping rain off ricks of hay.
It'll never happen because they were never there,

though I got it straight from the horse's mouth,
the boy who is the man who would have me
believe in a windfall borne to earth by silk,

in the hair's breadth we came to speaking German,
which is as close as I dare come to believing him.

South

On the outskirts of Rathkeale
a tree, in full leaf,
has given up the ghost.

∽

Bound with satin to a silver *Land Rover*,
white roses in the fast lane are borne easily south.

The horse in the horsebox it tows
gazes across the valley in disbelief.

∽

Someone has left, in Lyracrumpane,
the gate ajar for hares to escape.

∽

At Maamnahaltora 'The Star
Above the Garter' is my north star.

Even the gorse says *go mall*.

∽

The Gulf of Naples and Logavinshire,
where they penned and fed the horses,
are one and the same tonight.

We are Italians, opening Limoncello
and crushing the cap.

The night will be
as long as this bottle lasts.

Just after I open the door of the Gents
on the quay and just before I enter

the west wind slips in ahead of me
and sets off both hand dryers.

On a varnished partition
An Bíobla Naofa is balancing
between judgement and counsel.

It could go either way.
The slightest touch is all it takes.

Someone should swear in
the accordion and the accordion player
in the witness box whose tunes
will be their testimony.

The Courthouse, Féile na Bealtaine,
Dingle, May Day 2017

Dingle

for Fiona

I've put a country and a night between us.
The only words I can get out
are the names of ships —

*Papillon, Mám an Óraigh, Master Jack,
Chaos, Freebird, Sleeping Giant,
Realt na Mara, Starfisher, Oceanis.*

The fairest vessel in the harbour bears your name.

Acknowledgements and Notes

Acknowledgements are due to the editors of the following publications where a number of these poems, or versions of them, were published first: *2017 Saint Paul Almanac, A Bittern Cry* (The Francis Ledwidge Museum, Poetry Ireland/Éigse Eireann and Meath County Council, 2017), *Cyphers, The Honest Ulsterman, Navan: Its People & Its Past* (Vol. 4), *Poetry Ireland Review, The Stony Thursday Book* and *The Tangerine Magazine*.

The award of a bursary by An Chomhairle Ealaíon/The Arts Council, Ireland, in 2016 greatly facilitated this work. I am indebted too to the Tyrone Guthrie Centre at Annaghmakerrig for its legendary hospitality.

Grateful acknowledgement is also due to Solstice Arts Centre (Navan) and Cavan Arts Office (particularly Gerry Hennessy) for a *Cois Tine* Soundscapes Residency in Derrywinny, County Cavan in January 2017.

The frontispiece, a photograph (1917) of Heywood, Co Laois, by A E Henson is from Country Life Picture Library.

> page 22   *Schlüsselhalter,* keyholder
> page 28   Derrywinny, *Doire-bhainne* (The oak grove of the milk) — a grove where cows used to be milked. (P W Joyce, *Irish Names of Places*, Vol. I, 1871)
> page 56   The epigraph is Alexander Pope's principle of garden design — 'Consult the spirit of the place in all' — drawn from his 'Epistle 4 to Richard Boyle, Earl of Burlington', and is engraved on a pedestal in Lutyens' garden at Heywood.
> page 77   This poem gets its start from the sleeve notes for the tune titled 'The Further In the Deeper' on the recording *North* by Conor Caldwell and Danny Diamond.
> page 78   The Seaforth Highlanders of Canada disembarked in France on 13 August 1916 and fought as part of the 12th Infantry Brigade, 4th Canadian Division in France and Flanders until the end of the war.
> page 97   Logavinshire, *Log-a'-mhainseír* (Hollow of the manger) — where horses were penned in and fed. (Joyce, Vol. III)